Bears

Preschool/Kindergarten

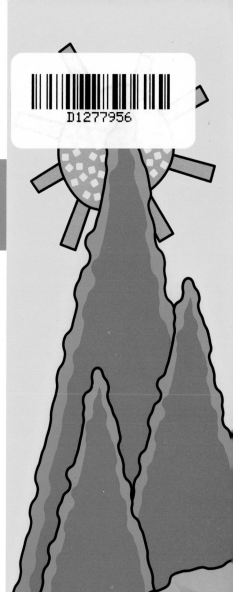

Save time and energy planning thematic units with this comprehensive resource. We've searched through the 1990–1997 issues of *The Mailbox®* and *Teacher's Helper®* magazines to find the best ideas for you to use when teaching a thematic unit on bears. Included in this book are favorite units from the magazines, single ideas to extend a unit, and a variety of reproducible activities. Pick and choose from these activities to develop your own complete unit or to simply enhance your current lesson plans. You're sure to find everything you need right here in this book to create a fun, integrated unit that will please you and your little cubs!

Editors:
Angie Kutzer
Michele M. Dare

Artists:
Cathy Spangler Bruce
Kimberly Richard

Cover Artist:
Kimberly Richard

www.themailbox.com

©1999 by THE EDUCATION CENTER, INC.
All rights reserved.
ISBN10 # 1-56234-318-1 • ISBN13 #978-156234-318-7

Manufactured in the United States
10 9 8 7 6 5

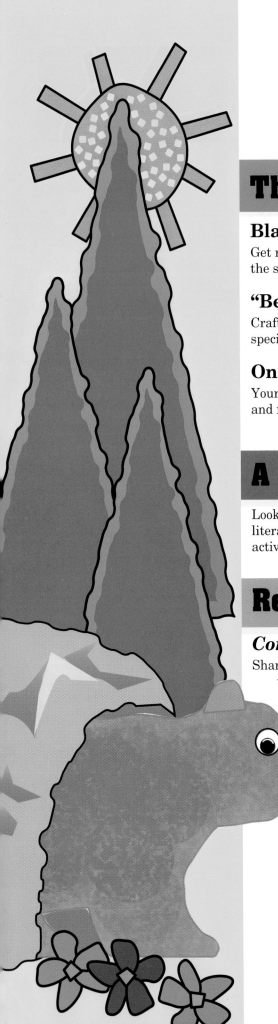

Table Of Contents

Thematic Units

Reproducible Activities

Thematic Units...

from The MAILBOX® Magazine.

Black Bear's Winter

Tracking down bear facts can be quite an enlightening experience for your budding nature lovers. Using the ideas in this unit, youngsters will have lots of opportunities to sing, sort, write, draw, and create their way to a better understanding of Black Bears and how they cope with winter weather.

by Lucia Kemp Henry

Black Bears live in dense brushlands and woodlands throughout most of North America. Compared to their relatives, Brown Bears and Polar Bears, Black Bears are the smallest. Adult males, called *boars,* can weigh up to 550 pounds. Adult females, called *sows,* weigh up to 300 pounds. Not all Black Bears are black in color. Some are brown, some are a reddish cinnamon-like color, and some are nearly white.

The Similarities Are Striking!

Read aloud one chapter at a time from *Black Bear Baby* by Berniece Freschet. At the conclusion of each chapter, find out what students learned about bear cubs. Encourage them to pinpoint things that cubs do that children also do. For example, bears like to wrestle and children sometimes like to wrestle too. Make a list of the ways that students believe bears and children are similar as you continue reading *Black Bear Baby*. Then ask for student volunteers to illustrate human and bear versions of each similarity.

All In The Family

Use the patterns on page 8 to make three bear families. Reproduce the patterns on white construction paper. Color one family of bears black, one family brown, and one reddish-brown. Cut out the bear patterns and prepare them for flannelboard use. Have your youngsters help you sort the families by color and display them in family groups on a flannelboard. After explaining the different names that are given to the males, females, and their offspring, ask your youngsters to point out the boars, the sows, and the cubs. Then ask students to re-sort the bears into these three categories. Conclude this activity by having each student draw and paint (or color) bears in a forest scene.

I like to climb trees.

Cubs climb trees too!

Barry Slate

Black Bears prepare for winter by eating as much food as they can find. They eat both plant and animal foods including berries, nuts, tubers, grains, fruits, small mammals, and insects—including bees.

Black Bears also select and prepare their dens for winter. They may use caves, hollow logs, and stumps which they supply with nest materials, such as moss, leaves, grass, and evergreen boughs. A female carefully selects and prepares a den that will be safe—not only for herself—but for her cubs too. A male may just lie down against a sheltering stump or log where he will be partially covered by an insulating blanket of snow.

When bears hibernate, they sleep for months without eating, drinking, or eliminating wastes from their bodies. They can wake up and move around their dens while in this period of winter rest.

Bear Is Sleeping
(sung to the tune of "Frère Jacques")

Bear is **sleeping.** Bear is **sleeping.**
Let it snow! Let it snow!
Sleeping all the winter, **sleeping** all the
    winter.
Snug and warm, snug and warm.

Repeat the song three more times, substituting in turn one of these words for the word *sleeping* each time it appears: *resting, napping,* and *snoring.*

Preparations For Winter

Delight your youngsters by suggesting that they make shape booklets that tell about a Black Bear's winter. Provide each youngster with a white construction-paper copy of each of the booklet patterns on pages 9–13. Ask each youngster to cut out her set of pages and staple them in order near the left edge. Following the suggestions for each page, have each student complete the booklet.

Directions For Booklet Pages:
Page One: Draw and color food beneath the bear. Draw berries, nuts, fruits, and insects. Color and complete the page as desired.
Page Two: Draw and color a cave or a hollow log in the open space. Color and complete the page as desired.
Page Three: Draw and color nest materials such as leaves and grass. Color and complete the page as desired.
Page Four: Draw and color a sleeping bear in the cave. Color and complete the page as desired.

Sleeping Bears

Snoozing, student-made Black Bears are the subject of this wintry bulletin board. To make a bear similar to the ones shown below, begin by coloring two 2 1/2-inch circle cutouts for the ears and by coloring the bottom of a paper nut cup for a muzzle. Remember that Black Bears can be black, brown, or reddish-brown. Then color the back of a thin paper plate using the same color. Referring to the illustration, glue the circular ears and the nut-cup muzzle onto the paper plate. Crumple a square of black tissue paper into a ball about the size of a walnut, and glue the ball of paper to the bottom of the nut cup to represent the bear's nose. To complete the snoozing bear, attach fringed, black construction-paper scraps to the paper plate to represent the bear's eyelashes. Encourage students to display their bear look-alikes on a bulletin board featuring a flurry of circular, sponge-printed snowflakes or student-made snowflake cutouts.

Asleep Under The Snow

How Do They Do It?

How many of your youngsters think that they would like to snooze the winter away just the way that bears do? Ask your students to imagine for a few moments that they are bears. What would their favorite sleeping positions be? Stimulate lively thoughts and discussions by reading aloud *How Do Bears Sleep?* by E. J. Bird. Then encourage students to imaginatively role-play as you reread the story. Whenever you mention a particular sleeping pose, pause to allow students to act out the position described. When you reach the part about the bear's dreams, encourage students to envision the images described.

Afterward give each child a copy of page 15. Ask each child to imagine that he's a bear and draw himself asleep in the cave. Encourage students to think about their favorite sleeping positions and name the things that help them drift off to sleep. Invite students to imaginatively complete their drawings to show the settings that would be most conducive to their sleep. After giving each student an opportunity to share his illustration with the class, bind the pages into a class book titled "Bedding Down For The Winter."

Big Old Bear

Convert the three-dimensional bear faces described in "Sleeping Bears" into masks by attaching a tongue depressor to the back of each bear likeness. These bear masks will be wonderful props to use when acting out the poem that follows:

Big Old Bear is nice and fat.
Ready for a winter's nap.
Big Old Bear is fast asleep.
Safe inside her cave so deep.
Big Old Bear is toasty warm.
Snow that falls can do no harm.
Big Old Bear is in her den.
When it's spring, she'll roam again.

by Lucia Kemp Henry

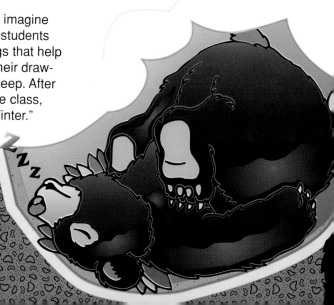

Where Is Bear Sleeping?

Rustle up a few teddy bears to set the stage for this cooperative group activity. Tie a ribbon of a different color around each bear's neck before "hiding" it either *on* or *in* some classroom object. Divide students into small groups and assign each group a different color to match one of the ribbon colors that you used. Ask each group of youngsters to find its sleeping bear—but not to move the bear. When a group has located its bear, give the group a copy of the sentence strip from page 14 that says, "Where is the bear sleeping?" Ask each group to discuss the location of its bear; then give the group the two remaining sentence strips from page 14. Ask if the bear is *on* or *in* something. If possible, have a student use an instant camera to photograph the group's bear. (If a camera is not available, have a student draw a picture of where the bear is located.) Attach the photo (or drawing) to the correct sentence strip to complete the sentence. Encourage each group to share its completed sentence strip with the other groups.

The is sleeping **in** the

Bedding Down

If you're talking about bears, you won't want to miss this fictional account of a bear that was having some trouble hibernating. Read aloud *Good Morning, Granny Rose* by Warren Ludwig. Then ask youngsters what things help them sleep comfortably. Some of the things that may be mentioned include night-lights, teddy bears, blankets, and soothing music. Make a large graph featuring your students' sleeping aids, and have each student put a personalized name or photo card in the column which represents his favorite sleeping aid. Make similar cards for Granny Rose, Henry, and the bear. Ask student volunteers to place these cards on the graph where they suspect that the cards should be. Encourage students to interpret the completed graph and comment on the results.

A Den Full Of Bear Books

Bearman
Written by Laurence Pringle
Photographed by Lynn Rogers
Published by Charles Scribner's Sons

Black Bear Baby
Written by Berniece Freschet
Illustrated by Jim Arnosky
Published by G. P. Putnam's Sons

Good Morning, Granny Rose
Written & Illustrated by Warren Ludwig
Published by G. P. Putnam's Sons

How Do Bears Sleep?
Written & Illustrated by E. J. Bird
Published by Carolrhoda Books, Inc.

Nature's Children: Black Bears
Written by Caroline Greenland
Published by Grolier

Eyewitness Juniors: Amazing Bears
Written by Theresa Greenaway
Photographed by Dave King
Published by Alfred A. Knopf, Inc.

Every Autumn Comes The Bear
Written & Illustrated by Jim Arnosky
Published by G. P. Putnam's Sons

Bears In The Forest
Written by Karen Wallace
Illustrated by Barbara Firth
Published by Candlewick Press

Alaska's Three Bears
Written by Shelley Gill
Illustrated by Shannon Cartwright
Published by Paws IV Publishing Company

Bear Family Patterns
Use with "All In The Family" on page 4.

boar

sow

cubs

©The Education Center, Inc. • *Bears* • Preschool/Kindergarten • TEC3184

Black Bear's Winter

by

©The Education Center, Inc. • *Bears* • Preschool/Kindergarten • TEC3184

The bear eats and eats before winter comes.
She won't need to eat again until spring.

©The Education Center, Inc. • *Bears* • Preschool/Kindergarten • TEC3184

1

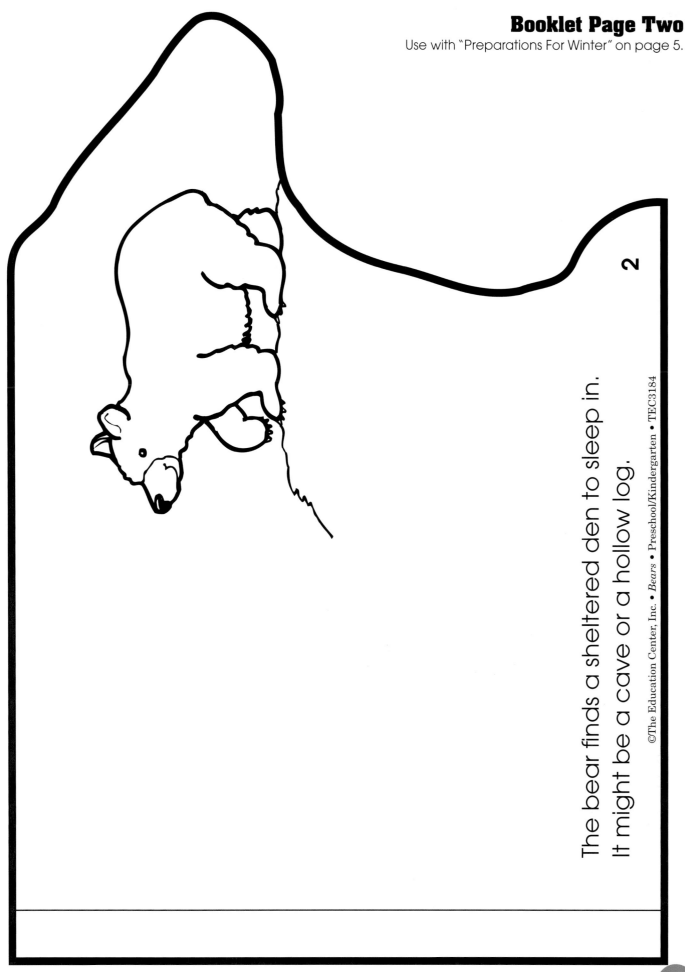

2

The bear finds a sheltered den to sleep in.
It might be a cave or a hollow log.

©The Education Center, Inc. • *Bears* • Preschool/Kindergarten • TEC3184

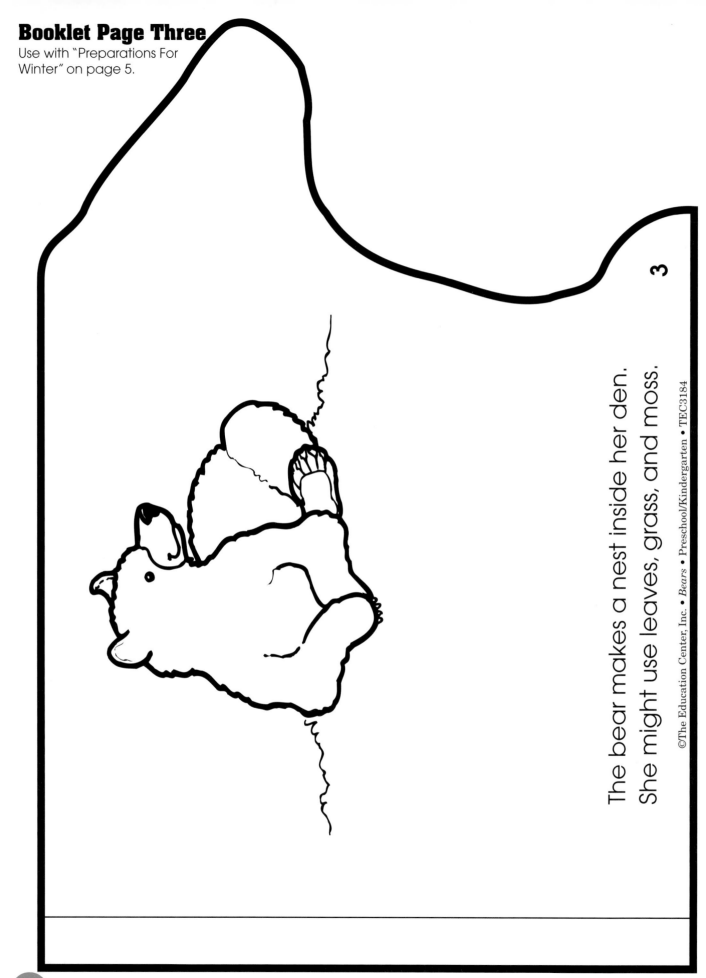

3

The bear makes a nest inside her den. She might use leaves, grass, and moss.

4

The bear sleeps in her den for most of the cold winter.

Rebus Sentence Strips

Use with "Where Is Bear Sleeping?" on page 7.

Where is the 🐻 sleeping?

The 🐻 is sleeping **on** the

The 🐻 is sleeping **in** the

_____ **Bear**
student's name
is sleeping.
Please be very quiet!

"BEAR" ESSENTIALS

If dreary days are more than you can bear, here are some great activities that will make them "bear-y" special. You'll find all the essentials for a fun-filled bear unit—activities to use with classic bear tales, a reading incentive program, and special party ideas.

A. A. Milne's Birthday

As an introduction to the unit, celebrate A. A. Milne's birthday, January 18. As your youngsters view a Winnie-the-Pooh videotape or listen to one of Milne's Pooh stories, serve teddy bear-shaped graham crackers and apple juice.

Corduroy Connection

After reading Don Freeman's *Corduroy* aloud, encourage students to explain Jenny's feelings about Corduroy. After the discussion, have each child draw a picture of his most-beloved toy. Then ask each child to dictate a sentence to you about his favorite toy. Write his sentence at the bottom of his illustration, and feature the illustrations in a display entitled "We Couldn't Bear To Be Without These Toys."

"Bear-y" Good Readers

Here's a reading incentive program that encourages students and parents to read at home together. Begin the incentive program by introducing it to parents. To do this, duplicate a copy of the note to parents on page 18 and five copies of the parent verification form on page 18 for each child. Staple the note and verification forms together and send them home with each child prior to the beginning of the program. Duplicate additional copies of the verification form, staple them in sets of five, and distribute them to students as needed throughout the program.

Progress Puzzles

Give students the big picture of their reading progress with this display idea. Duplicate two copies of the bear on page 19 for each student. Label each of the student's two bears with his name. Mount one on construction paper, and display it on a bulletin board entitled "We Are 'Bear-y' Good Readers." Have him color his remaining bear and cut it out on the bold outline. Cut each child's bear into 20 pieces using the guidelines on the pattern. Store his cut-out pieces in an envelope or Ziploc® bag labeled with his name. Each time a child brings a completed verification form to school, allow him to select a colored piece from his envelope or bag to glue in the appropriate place on his displayed bear outline. Your students will enjoy piecing their bears together as their reading progress grows.

Pom-Pom Bear Bookmarks

Reward each " 'Bear-y' Good Reader" with a special bookmark he can make himself. For each bookmark you'll need: a tongue depressor; a medium-sized, light brown pom-pom; three small, dark brown pom-poms; a miniature black pom-pom; and a permanent marker. Use a permanent marker to write a message on the tongue depressor as shown. Assist each recipient in gluing the pom-poms onto his tongue depressor to resemble a teddy bear's head. Add the bear's eyes using permanent marker. With great bookmarks like these, children will be anxious to read even more books!

Broadway Bears

Your students will enjoy taking center stage in their own reenactment of *Goldilocks And The Three Bears*. Using paper plates, make masks resembling Goldilocks and each of the three bears as shown. Tie elastic thread through holes punched in the sides of each mask. Provide additional props such as bowls, spoons, a table, chairs, and mats or blankets to use as beds.

As you read the story orally, have students take turns wearing the masks and portraying Goldilocks and each of the three bears. As a follow-up activity, provide additional paper plates and cutouts so each child can make a mask resembling his favorite character from the story. Watch your little stars shine as they are magically transformed into these fairy-tale characters.

Teddy Bear Tea Party

Conclude your teddy bear unit with this gala celebration. Duplicate the invitation on page 20 for each child and distribute copies the day before the party. Provide extra teddy bears for students who forget or are unable to bring them to school. Invite the teddies to share in all of the usual daily activities. Even nap time is more fun when it's shared with the teddies. During center time, have youngsters assemble a teddy bear cake from one large, round layer; one small, round layer; and six cupcakes as shown. Have youngsters frost the teddy bear cake with chocolate icing, and use M & M's®, jelly beans, and licorice laces to make facial features. Serve the cake along with Kool-Aid® using teddy bear cups and napkins.

"Teddy-cademy" Awards

Use the pattern on page 18 to make a necklace award for each teddy bear tea party guest. Duplicate the pattern on construction paper for each teddy, punch a hole in the top of each award, and tie a piece of yarn or ribbon through it to make a necklace. During the party, ask each child to share something about his bear with the class as you complete the awards. Some award suggestions are: "Biggest Bear," "Oldest Bear," "Funniest Bear," and "Most-loved Bear." At the end of the party, announce the winners and present each teddy with his award.

Most-loved Bear

Teddy And Me Picture Frames

Help youngsters remember the teddy bear tea party for years to come by making this special keepsake. Photograph each child and his award-winning teddy. Using the pattern on page 20, make a construction paper frame for each child's photo. Tie colorful ribbon into bows. Place the bows on the frames as either hair bows for girls or bow ties for boys. Your students will be thrilled with these "bear-y" special momentos of the day.

Teddy and Me

ideas by: Susan Keith, Fairview Elementary, St. Louis, MO
DeAnna Lederle—Pre/K, Milford, NJ
Kaye Sowell—Gr. K, Pelahatchie Elementary, Pelahatchie, MS

Note To Parents

Use with "'Bear-y' Good Readers" on page 16.

Dear Parent,

As you know, reading to your child is essential in the development of his prereading skills. To help encourage reading at home, our class is starting an incentive program entitled " 'Bear-y' Good Readers." Each time you read a book with your child, please fill out a verification form and return it to school. Your child will receive a "bear-y" special reward when he has read 20 books. Thank you for your support of this program.

Sincerely,

_____

©The Education Center, Inc. • *Bears* • Preschool/Kindergarten • TEC3184

Parent Verification Form

Use with "'Bear-y' Good Readers" on page 16.

Pattern

Use with "'Teddy-cademy' Awards" on page 17.

I'm helping _____

become a

"Bear-y" Good Reader!

We read together last night.

date: _____

signed: _____

©The Education Center, Inc.

©The Education Center, Inc.

is a
"Bear-y"
Good
Reader!

Invitation

Use with "Teddy Bear Tea Party" on page 17.

You're invited to a
Teddy Bear Tea Party!

**Bring your favorite teddy bear to school
with you tomorrow for a day of fun.**

Pattern

Use with "Teddy And Me Picture Frames" on page 17.

Cut out this space.
Attach a photograph to the
back of this frame.

Teddy and Me

Once Upon A Bear

A Whole Language Treasury
Of Books About Bears

"There is no substitute for real books. They are rarely boring or sanitized or squeezed into a 'reading system' that children can smell a mile off. So logic says if we want real readers we must give them real books; give our young people good literature, good art, and surprisingly, these young people may do the rest."

Tomie dePaola

reprinted with permission from *Children's Literature In The Reading Program;* Bernice E. Cullinan, Editor; copyright 1987 by the International Reading Association, Inc.

Jamberry by Bruce Degen

Get buried in berries. In this delightful rhyming book, a boy and a bear have one amazing berry episode after another. Luscious pictures with humorous details make this book a feast for the eyes and ears.

Caution: reading this book may give kids the urge to get elbow deep in jamberries. So divide your class into four groups and set up four finger-painting stations, each supplied with a color of fingerpaint and wet fingerpaint paper. Provide blue paint for blueberries, red paint for strawberries, purple paint for blackberries, and red paint tinted with a little blue for raspberries. When the fingerpaintings are dry, trace (or have students trace) corresponding, oversize, berry-shaped patterns onto them and cut out. Display a cascade of these fruit cutouts on a bulletin board along with the students' own version of a *Jamberry* verse.

In Bruce Degen's letter at the end of *Jamberry,* he describes berry picking when he was a youngster. Share this letter; then find out if your students have ever picked berries. If possible, go on a berry-picking field trip. If not, bring in fresh blueberries, blackberries, strawberries, and/or raspberries from a supermarket. Have youngsters clean and sample the fresh fruit. Then serve it as Bruce Degen remembered it, with sour cream and sugar. As you are sampling the fruit, ask your students to describe special times spent working with their grandparents or elderly friends. Encourage students to compare and contrast time-consuming, "old-fashioned" methods of gathering and preparing foods to more rapid "convenience" methods popular today.

The Bear's Toothache by David McPhail

Your youngsters will giggle with delight at the unfolding antics in this story about a bear with a toothache and the boy who befriends him. Share this book when a student loses a tooth or as an introduction to dental health discussions.

Vivid imaginary escapades unfold in this delightful tale. Have your students recount all the ways the boy and the bear attempted to pull the aching tooth. What other things would your students have tried? Find out if your students have ever "pulled" one of their baby teeth. What imaginative techniques did they consider to get the tooth out? On a giant tooth cutout, list several of the tooth-pulling techniques mentioned.

Have students take another look at the last picture. Have them speculate on the reason why the tooth is under the pillow. On chart paper, write a student-dictated letter from the tooth fairy concerning the giant tooth.

The Bear's Toothache is full of opposites. The bear was *outside,* then *inside.* The bear is *big,* and the boy is *little.* The bear's mouth is shown both *open* and *closed.* The kitchen is *dark* with the exception of the refrigerator, which is *light.* The boy was *awake;* his dad must have been *asleep.* The bear was *up* high in the window, until he jumped *down.* Provide a tooth-shaped cutout for each student to string onto a yarn necklace. On his cutout, have him write a word (such as those italicized above) from the story; then have him write its opposite on the back.

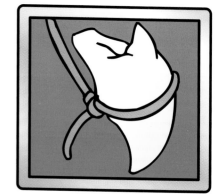

Fix-It by David McPhail

In light of information concerning the negative impact of television viewing and the positive effects of reading as an alternative to television, this acclaimed book is one you won't want to miss. Follow it up with further adventures of Emma in *Emma's Pet* and *Emma's Vacation.*

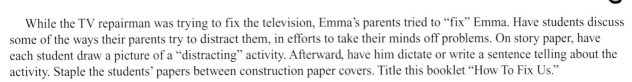

Watching television must have become a reflex for Emma. Find out when and why your students usually watch television. Have students discuss fun and productive things to do instead of watching television. List each activity beside a related picture clue. Duplicate the list for each student, and ask students to keep the lists near their television sets. Whenever they're tempted to turn on the tube, encourage them to first check the list to see if there isn't something more exciting to do.

While the TV repairman was trying to fix the television, Emma's parents tried to "fix" Emma. Have students discuss some of the ways their parents try to distract them, in efforts to take their minds off problems. On story paper, have each student draw a picture of a "distracting" activity. Afterward, have him dictate or write a sentence telling about the activity. Staple the students' papers between construction paper covers. Title this booklet "How To Fix Us."

Big Bad Bruce by Bill Peet

Bruce was a huge bully of a bear. Until—that is—he bullied the wrong person. Because this book is lengthy, consider ending the first read-aloud session after page 19. Before finishing the book in a later session, serve some blueberry pie and have students recall the events that have already transpired.

Do your students know anyone who gets a kick out of scaring people—especially people smaller than himself? Have students role-play a situation involving a bully. Then discuss what could cause a person to act this way. Ask students what would happen if the roles were suddenly reversed? Serve (or pretend to serve) some blueberry pie. Have your students role-play a situation in which the bully has become little and defenseless, and someone much bigger is picking on him. What have your students learned about bullying?

In *Big Bad Bruce,* the witch, who originally seemed hard and hateful, turned out to be kindly and gentle. Find out if your youngsters ever had a dim opinion of someone until they got to know him better. Explain that the more you know about someone, the more there is to like about him. Have each student choose a person (other than a classmate) that he knows rather well. Using a paper plate, glue, tissue paper, scissors, and miscellaneous art supplies, have each student convert the paper plate into a likeness of the person he's selected. After the artwork is dry, staple each likeness to a bulletin board with two or three student-dictated positive comments about the person.

Blackboard Bear by Martha Alexander

The inside front cover says it beautifully: "It's hard to be small in a big kids' world unless you have a friend like Blackboard Bear." Your youngsters will delight both in the sweet revenge of a little guy just about their size and in his enchanted bear companion. Read the further adventures of Anthony and his bear in *And My Mean Old Mother Will Be Sorry, Blackboard Bear; I Sure Am Glad To See You, Blackboard Bear;* and *We're In Big Trouble, Blackboard Bear.*

Cause your youngsters to reflect on their past experiences which parallel those of the main character. Begin reading *Blackboard Bear,* but stop after the page on which the police officer tells the little boy to, "Go play with your teddy bear." Ask what similar things they have experienced that help them relate to the main character's dilemma. Finish the book, giving children ample time to examine the illustrations and absorb the ironic conclusion. Find out how they feel about the way the story ended; then have them brainstorm new endings to the story.

Delight your youngsters with a class blackboard bear. Or get a parent volunteer or older student to help you prepare a smaller, blackboard bear for each of your students. Using the illustrations from the book as a reference, create a bear-shaped tagboard pattern. To make a blackboard bear, trace your bear pattern onto green or black Con-Tact® paper. Cut out and mount the bear shape on a cardboard rectangle. Using a permanent white paint pen, add a few facial features. If desired, trim the cardboard around the bear outline, and add a red Con-Tact® covering collar and a red yarn "leash." Tape chalk to the free end of the leash. Then use the blackboard bear for related basic skills practice.

OLD BEAR by Jane Hissey

Rescuing Old Bear is more of a challenge than his four stuffed friends anticipate. But once your youngsters meet this fuzzy crew they'll be delighted to learn that their adventures continue. Follow up this story with Hissey's *Little Bear's Trousers* and *Old Bear Tales.*

Getting Old Bear out of the attic required all the problem-solving skills four fuzzy toys could muster. Have your students discuss each of the attempts to reach the attic door. Point out the validity of each rescue attempt. Then have them plan a similar rescue mission, but this time the attempt would have to be made using things available in their

own bedrooms or play areas. What innovative means do your students propose for the rescue? Have each student illustrate his idea on story paper and dictate or write about this new rescue mission. Staple these papers into a booklet to be displayed in your reading area. With the help of students, simulate the most popular rescue missions using stuffed toys and the props mentioned in their papers.

Rekindle an old friendship, just as the characters in *Old Bear* did. Find out how your youngsters feel when they lose touch with a friend. Have students name some of the best ways to get in touch with distant friends. Then help students send a letter or (student-made) gift to a student or faculty member who has moved away or who has not been heard from for a while. If appropriate, send along a copy of *Old Bear* and a letter explaining that your students hope to rekindle their friendship just as the animals in *Old Bear* rekindled theirs.

Where's My Daddy?

adapted from a story by Shigeo Watanabe

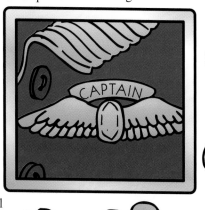

Of the "I Can Do It All By Myself" series *School Library Journal* asserts, "These lovely books are true boosters for preschool confidence, self-concept, and beginning reading skills." In *Where's My Daddy?*, one of the titles in this nine-book series, Bear discovers that perseverance pays off.

Bear finds his daddy all by himself. What things can your youngsters do all by themselves? Make a list. How does doing things on their own make them feel? Give each student a large T-shirt cut from pastel art paper. On the cutout, have each student illustrate one thing he can do for himself if he perseveres. Then, on the cutout, have him dictate a completion for and copy this sentence: I can _____ all by myself. Using clothespins, hang all the T-shirt cutouts on a clothesline pinned to a bulletin board. Add the title "We Can Do It All By Ourselves."

Most grown-ups stay busy. So they don't always stop what they're doing to help a little person who has the situation under control. In the book, the cat was running from the dog, the milk goat was delivering milk, the hippo was delivering newspapers, the donkey was delivering letters, and Mommy was hanging wash out to dry. Using an opaque projector, project several pages from Richard Scarry's *Busiest People Ever* for students to examine. After deciding on a career that interests him, have each student illustrate himself in that role. Staple the pages between construction paper covers, and display this book in your reading corner.

First Flight by David McPhail

As a youngster embarks on his first airplane flight—bear in hand—he's off for quite an adventure. Read this book after an airport field trip. It meshes the real and the imagined in a way that is certain to delight your youngsters. If your youngsters cry for more of the same, read aloud *The Bear's Bicycle* by Emilie Warren McLeod.

Take your students aboard an airplane. Or, if boarding the real thing is out of the question, take your students aboard an imaginary airplane. In advance, have students bring in pictures of places they'd like to visit. (Provide some travel brochures for variety.) Align chairs in rows of two or three to represent an airplane. After voting on a destination and checking its location on a map, dramatize the entire flight, from buying the tickets to speaking to the captain on the way out. Interview each of your youngsters on videotape, asking him to describe part of his flight (or airport field trip) for a news broadcast.

It's always challenging to do something you've never done before. Other than flying, have your students name some things they've never done before. Make a list. What fears or uncertainties do they have about making their first attempts? If some of your students have attempted things on the list, how do they feel about having tried them? Provide magazines and catalogs, and have students locate and cut out pictures and words representing things they've never tried. Assist students in gluing the cutouts to a bulletin board to create a collage. Students who have tried the activities may attach colorful wing cutouts to the board.

And They Read Bear Books Happily Ever After.

We're Going On A Bear Hunt
retold by Michael Rosen
The old favorite slap-tap-and-clap chant is now a children's book. If desired, use this book to introduce your youngsters to the world of bear books. After all, tracking down bear books can be just as much fun as hunting for the real thing!

Goldilocks And The Three Bears
by Jan Brett
Children never tire of traditional fairy tales. So be sure and read them this beautiful rendition of *The Three Bears.*

Goodbye House
by Frank Asch
For your students who have moved or will soon be moving, *Goodbye House* is a soothing treatment for an unsettling time. Other books by Frank Asch which feature bear characters include: *Bear Shadow; Bear's Bargain; Bread And Honey; Happy Birthday, Moon!; Just Like Daddy; Moon Bear; Mooncake; Moongame;* and *Sand Cake.*

Blueberries For Sal
by Robert McCloskey
Pass around the blueberries as you read this Caldecott Award Honor Book about a blueberry-picking little girl and a blueberry-picking bear cub who end up following the wrong mothers.

Little Bear
by Else Holmelund Minarik
This book, the first in a series of easy readers, is a timeless classic. Follow up its reading with *A Kiss For Little Bear, Father Bear Comes Home, Little Bear's Friend,* and *Little Bear's Visit* (A Caldecott Award Honor Book).

The Three Bears Rhyme Book
by Jane Yolen
During your bear unit, keep a copy of this poetry collection nearby. After all, what better way is there to fill a spare minute than with a "bear-y" good poem?

. . A Den Full Of Ideas . .

Bouncing Bear

Your little ones will learn to work together with this group movement activity. Space your children evenly around a parachute or a large sheet. Instruct each child to hold the parachute tightly with both hands. Next place a teddy bear in the center of the parachute and challenge the children to move their hands so that the bear bounces and flips in the air, rolls from one side of the parachute to the other side, and rolls in a circle around the parachute. Hurrah for teamwork!

Susan Burbridge—Four-Year-Olds
Trinity Weekday School
San Antonio, TX

Refrigerator Art

If you're into recycling, you're going to love these student-made magnets made from Styrofoam® trays. In advance press a bear cookie cutter into a Styrofoam tray, and cut around the imprinted design using an X-acto® knife. To convert the bear cutout into a decorative magnet, paint the front and sides of the bear with gesso. (This prepares a nice base for the paint.) Paint the bear. When the paint has dried, add wiggle eyes, a bow, and marker details. To complete this "bear-y" cute refrigerator magnet, attach a self-adhesive magnet strip to the back of the cutout.

Julie Mead—Gr. K
Lewis, KS

Little Bear And The Bee

Bears love honey...but so do bees!

Little bear, little bear, up in the tree.

Little bear, little bear, looking down at me.

Little bear, little bear, can't you see?

Little bear, little bear, here comes a bee!

Linda Ludlow, Pittsboro, IN

Bear Claws

Use this special recipe when learning about bears or the letter *b*. To create a bear claw, you will need: a can of biscuits, margarine (melted), cinnamon sugar, and almond slivers. To make a bear claw, cook biscuits according to package directions. Brush each biscuit with the melted margarine; then sprinkle with cinnamon sugar. While the biscuit is still very warm, insert five almond slivers around the edge of the biscuit so it looks like a bear claw.

Betty Lynn Scholtz—Gr. K, St. Ann's School, Charlotte, NC

Share Bear

A special teddy bear will add a sense of closure to your end-of-the-day circle time. Designate a favorite stuffed teddy as "Share Bear." When you gather students at the end of the day, give each child an opportunity to hold Share Bear and describe a favorite activity of that day. Each youngster will leave your care with a happy memory to then share with Mom or Dad!

Elaine M. Utt—Two-Year-Olds
La Petite Academy, Tampa, FL

Hibernation Song

This sweet song is about sleeping. But if youngsters perform the motions while singing the song, you won't have any trouble keeping everyone awake. Request that the children sing the first and third verses with moderately loud voices, and the second verse with quiet voices.

(sung to the tune of "Are You Sleeping?")

Are you eating,	*Pretend to eat with paws.*
Are you eating,	
Little bear?	*Hold hand down, palm flat.*
Little bear?	
Eating nuts and berries,	*Pretend to eat with paws.*
For the long, hard winter,	*Shiver and rub arms.*
Little bear.	*Hold hand down, palm flat.*
Little bear.	

Are you sleeping,	*Lay head on hands.*
Are you sleeping,	
Little bear?	*Hold hand down, palm flat.*
Little bear?	
Sleeping through the winter,	*Lay head on hands.*
You are hibernating,	
Little bear.	*Hold hand down, palm flat.*
Little bear.	

Are you waking,	*Stretch and pretend to yawn.*
Are you waking,	
Little bear?	*Hold hand down, palm flat.*
Little bear?	
Now that it is springtime,	*Hop up and down.*
Sleeping time is over,	*Point finger back and forth.*
Little bear.	*Hold hand down, palm flat.*
Little bear.	

Linda Ludlow—Preschool, Bethesda Christian Schools, Brownsburg, IN

Much Ado About Hibernation

Studying hibernation? Then your youngsters will take special pride in creating this hibernator's haven. To make this cave project, place a brown paper grocery bag on a tabletop so that the folded bottom of the bag is faceup. Cut the bag off about one inch below the folded bottom. Then unfold the bag bottom and cut a *u*-shaped opening from one side. Place the bag bottom so that one side rests flat on the table and the side with the *u*-shaped opening rests at an angle, creating an imitation cave. Draw, color, and cut out plants and animals to decorate the cave. Glue them onto the bag.

Anna P. Dorcas
St. Andrew Preschool, Crosslanes, WV

We're Going On A Bear Hunt

Retold by Michael Rosen
Published by Simon & Schuster Children's Books

What's more fun than a bear hunt? With this clever craft idea, even your little ones will be able to retell the events of this popular book. To make a story bear, each child will need a large, construction-paper bear shape. Have him fringe a small strip of green paper, then glue it near the top of the bear to represent grass; then have him glue a small piece of blue streamer on the bear to represent the river. Next direct the child to paint brown paint to represent the mud, glue on several small paper tree shapes to represent the forest, and glue on small pieces of a white doily to represent the snowstorm. At the bottom of the bear shape, have him glue on a pom-pom bear. (To make a pom-pom bear, glue two brown pom-poms together; then add wiggle eyes, paper ears, and a paper nose.) If you have a miniature paw-print stamp, have each child stamp it on the bear shape as a finishing touch. We're going on a bear hunt. What's that? A BEAR!

Bonnie L. Wyke—Developmentally Delayed Three-Year-Olds
Charles W. Bush School, Wilmington, DE

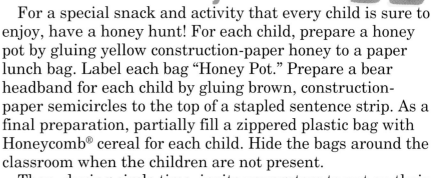

Honey Hunt

For a special snack and activity that every child is sure to enjoy, have a honey hunt! For each child, prepare a honey pot by gluing yellow construction-paper honey to a paper lunch bag. Label each bag "Honey Pot." Prepare a bear headband for each child by gluing brown, construction-paper semicircles to the top of a stapled sentence strip. As a final preparation, partially fill a zippered plastic bag with Honeycomb® cereal for each child. Hide the bags around the classroom when the children are not present.

Then, during circle time, invite youngsters to put on their bear headbands, pick up their honey pots, and forage for honey! As each child locates a plastic bag of cereal, encourage him to place it in his honey pot and return to the circle area. Then invite your hunters to eat their cereal snacks. Mmmm...I'm as hungry as a bear!

Linda Rice Ludlow—Four-Year-Olds
Bethesda Christian School, Brownsburg, IN

Read "Bear-y" Quietly

Make your reading center a delightful place for students to practice "reading" skills using a rocking chair and teddy bears. Place a basket of teddy bears beside a large rocking chair in your reading center. Invite students to snuggle up with a teddy and read "bear-y" quietly so only teddy can hear the story.

Sara Kennedy, Bedford, VA

Coffee Bears

This project is not only fun to make, but it is also a real sensory experience. To make a coffee bear, trace a bear pattern (or draw one yourself) on a sheet of brown construction paper; then cut on the resulting outline. Draw facial features on the bear. Next spread glue on portions of the bear to represent its stomach, ears, and paws. Then sprinkle dried coffee grounds atop the glue. When the glue dries, shake off the excess coffee grounds.

Sara Bockover—Gr. K, Keith Country Day School, Rockford, IL

Bear Family Visitors

A visit from the bear family makes learning fun! Fill a plastic school box with a family of plastic bear figurines, a small teddy bear, his blanket, flash cards, a book, and a journal. Program an index card for parents that tells them how to use the materials with their children, and tuck it inside the box. Each day, allow a different youngster to take the box home. With his parent's help, have the youngster complete the activities specified on the card, then dictate a journal entry about the bears' visit to his home. The next day, have the youngster share his journal entry with his classmates.

Jennifer Woods—Gr. K
Alma Primary
Alma, AR

May 18, 2000
I had fun with the bears. we read Corduroy. I took the bears for a bike ride.
Erin

I printed big and small bears.

"Beary" Big And "Beary" Small

Use a retelling of *Goldilocks And The Three Bears* along with this art project to emphasize the concepts of big and small. In advance, label each child's paper as shown. Using a die-cutting machine or a bear pattern, cut several large bear shapes and several small bear shapes from sponges. Have each child make large and small bear prints on his paper using the sponges and brown paint. Assist him in counting the number of big and small bears that he printed on his paper. This activity is sure to be big fun for small hands.

Betsy Ruggiano—Three-Year-Olds
Featherbed Lane School, Clark, NJ

Color Bears

Use this activity during circle time to practice color recognition. In advance draw a teddy-bear face on different colors of construction paper; then cut on the resulting outlines to produce one bear per child. Laminate the bear faces if desired. Mount the bear cutouts on craft sticks. During group time, pass a bear to each child. Start by saying, "Yellow bear, yellow bear, what do you see?" Have the child or children holding the yellow bear(s) stand, look around the classroom, and identify items that are yellow. Continue in this manner until all of the colors have been called. "Color-ific!"

Martha Berry—Two-Year-Olds
Main Street United Methodist Preschool
Kernersville, NC

Tasty Teddy Bear Math

Teddy Grahams® turn patterning and graphing activities into delicious learning fun. Give each youngster a Ziploc® bag containing vanilla and chocolate Teddy Grahams and a paper plate. On his paper plate, have each youngster duplicate and/or complete a pattern you make. Or have him create patterns of his own. Have youngsters sample their crackers. Then have each youngster glue a cracker indicating his preference on a class graph. Have youngsters nibble on their remaining crackers as they discuss the results of the graph.

Cindy Stuart—Gr. K
North Sumter Jr. High School
Livingston, AL

Ten Bears In My Bed
by Stan Mack

Teddy Grahams® provide the manipulative magic for this activity. For each youngster, fold and staple a sheet of construction paper to form a pocket as shown. Have each youngster decorate his pocket to resemble a bed, then place ten Teddy Grahams on top of the "bed." Have youngsters join you in counting the number of bears; then, as you read the story aloud, have them manipulate their bears as indicated in the story. Each time another bear leaves the bed, pause to count the remaining bears. When the story is over, have each youngster tuck his bears in their bed before snacking on additional crackers and juice. As a follow-up, have youngsters take their teddy-filled beds home and tell the story to their families.

Lenora Meyer—Gr. K
Ezra Millard School, Omaha, NE

Teddy Bear Parade

This number-line strategy is a "beary" good way to reinforce numbers, colors, patterns, and skip counting. To implement this idea, you will need a bear cutout for each day that children attend school. Alternating between two different colors of paper, cut out a series of bears so that every fifth bear is significantly larger than the four that precede it. Number and display the bears sequentially so that they create a decorative border around your classroom. Each day, encourage your children to find the bear that matches the date or the number of the day in the school year. To practice skip counting, direct the children to say all of the numbers on blue bears, for example, or all of the numbers on the bigger bears.

Wilma Droegemueller—Grs. Preschool and K, Zion Lutheran School, Mt. Pulaski, IL

Color Bear Bags

These nifty color bears will help youngsters review color recognition. In advance, cut out pairs of bear shapes from different colors of construction paper. Glue one bear from each pair onto a white lunch bag. Open the bags and stand them in a row on the floor. Provide each child with a cutout. In turn, have each child identify the color of his bear and place it in the corresponding bag.

Debi Luke—Preschool, Fairmount Nursery School
Syracuse, NY

Teddy Bear Treats

Make some Corduroy cupcakes after reading the book. Decorate cupcakes with chocolate icing. To give them a fuzzy, bearlike look, dip them in a bowl of cookie crumbs. Use tubed icing to add facial features. Then poke round chocolate cookie miniatures into the icing for bear ears.

Lynette Pyne, Plainsboro, NJ

"Bear-y" Neat Dens

While learning about bears, youngsters will enjoy making these bear dens. For each child, cut off the top half of a plastic milk jug to represent a bear den; then cut a half circle on opposite sides of the den to create entrances. Have the child glue cotton balls over the outside of the den. After the glue dries, invite little ones to engage in some fun play using their dens and teddy-bear counters or cookies.

Nancy Kaczrowski, Luverne, MN

Teddy Bear Sleep-Over

During your bear unit, invite little ones to bring their favorite teddy bears to class for a sleep-over. Have students use the bears in a variety of activities—such as counting and sorting—as well as including them in their daily routines. Before they leave for the day, ask students to tuck their bears in for the night. Then move the bears to different areas of the room after students leave. When youngsters arrive the next day, they will be delighted to discover that their bears came to life overnight!

Deanna Evans—Gr. K
Richland, MO

Did You Nap Today?

Encourage your little nappers to catch some *z*'s with this fun incentive. At students' eye level, mount a laminated bed-shaped cutout on a wall of your room. Then mount a quilt-patterned border around the bed and attach a construction-paper pillow cutout atop the bed. For each child, personalize a laminated teddy-bear cutout. Cut one piece of self-adhesive Velcro® for each cutout. Attach the hook side of each Velcro® piece to the back of a bear cutout. Mount the loop side of each piece on the bed cutout. Place the teddy-bear cutouts near the display. Each day after naptime, have each child who napped place his teddy bear on the bed. Parents can check the display each day to see if their children caught some *z*'s!

Barb Young—Three-Year-Olds
Peace Memorial Child Care Center
Palos Park, IL

Reproducible Activities...

from Teachers Helper® Magazine.

Story Synopsis

Corduroy

Written by Don Freeman
Published by Viking Press

Corduroy is a sad little bear sitting on a toy department shelf. In his distinctive green overalls, he is anxiously waiting for someone special to come and buy him and take him home. One day, Lisa, a little girl, sees Corduroy and asks her mother if she can buy Corduroy. Her mother replies that since Corduroy is missing a button on his overalls, he isn't in good enough condition to buy. Corduroy sets out that evening, after the store closes, to find his missing button. Corduroy is intrigued with all that he sees in the department store, but the night guard finds him and returns him to the toy shelf before he can find a button to fix his overalls. Lisa returns to the store the next day and buys Corduroy with her own money. She takes him home and sews on a new button for his overalls, and the two new friends begin a wonderful relationship!

From *Corduroy* by Don Freeman ©1968.
Reprinted by permission of Penguin Putnam
Books for Young Readers.

How To Use Page 39

1. Read the story *Corduroy* or review the events of the story with your children before introducing this sheet. (See the story synopsis above.)
2. Encourage discussion about each picture on this worksheet.
3. Tell the children to color only those pictures that show something that happened in the story about Corduroy. *(Hint: Corduroy does not jump out of a present.)*

Finished sample

What happened to Corduroy?

Think.

Color.

Where Are The Buttons?

Find the buttons.

🖍 Color.

Fix up the bear in a special way,
so some little child will buy it today!

I can fix the bear. I can

by _____

41

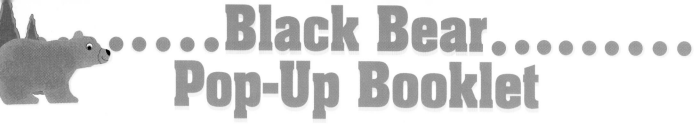

Black Bear Pop-Up Booklet

Background For The Teacher

Black bears live in dense brushlands and woodlands throughout most of North America. Compared to their relatives, brown bears and polar bears, black bears are the smallest. Adult males, called *boars,* can weigh up to 550 pounds. Adult females, called *sows,* weigh up to 300 pounds. Not all black bears are black in color. Some are brown; some are a reddish, cinnamonlike color; and some are nearly white.

Black bears prepare for winter by eating as much food as they can find. They eat both plant and animal foods including berries, nuts, tubers, grains, fruits, small mammals, and insects—such as bees.

Black bears also select and prepare their dens for winter. They may use caves, hollow logs, and stumps which they supply with nest materials such as moss, leaves, grass, and evergreen boughs. A female carefully selects and prepares a den that will be safe—not only for herself, but for her cubs too. A male may just lie down against a sheltering stump or log where he will be partially covered by an insulating blanket of snow.

When bears hibernate, they sleep for months without eating, drinking, or eliminating wastes from their bodies. They can wake up and move around their dens while in this period of winter rest.

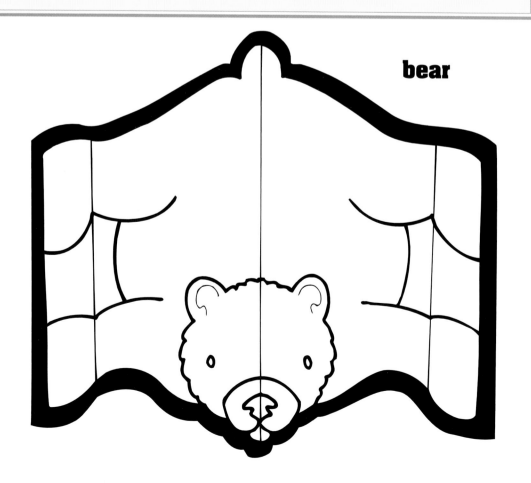

bear

Materials Needed For Each Child

— one copy each of pages 44–47 on white construction paper
— one copy of the bear pattern on page 42 on white construction paper
— scissors
— glue
— a pencil
— crayons
— two black buttons, felt circles, or wiggle eyes

How To Make A Black Bear Pop-Up Booklet Pages 44–47

1. To begin assembling the booklet, cut out the cover and the three booklet pages (pages 44–47) along the heavy outlines.
2. Glue booklet page 2 where indicated and attach it to the back of booklet page 1 so that the dotted lines meet. Then fold booklet page 1 along the double lines.
3. Glue the booklet cover to the back of booklet page 1.
4. Glue booklet page 3 to the back of booklet page 2.
5. To complete the front cover, color the bear. Glue two black buttons, felt circles, or wiggle eyes on the bear. Write your name in the space provided.
6. In the first box on booklet page 1, **draw and color a furry black bear.**
7. In the second box on booklet page 1, **draw and color nuts, berries, grass, and insects.**
8. In the first box on booklet page 2, **draw and color a sleeping bear.**
9. In the second box on booklet page 2, **draw a simple bear track.**
10. Color the bear pattern and cut it out.
11. See the illustration of the three-dimensional bear. Fold your bear similarly. Then glue the feet sections where indicated.
12. Read booklet page 3. Color the bear pictures to show the different colors of black bears. Write some words to describe black bears.

Front

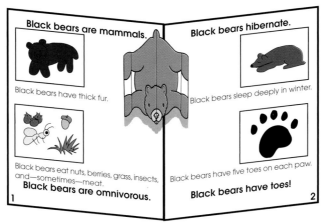

Inside

Back

My Black Bear Book

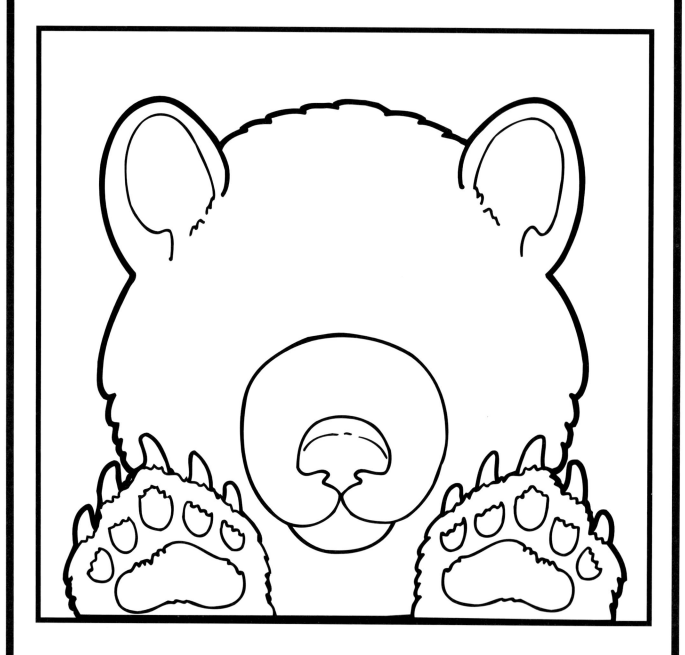

by

Black bears are mammals.

Glue bear's feet here.

Black bears have thick fur.

← Fold here. ↑

Black bears eat nuts, berries, grass, insects, and—sometimes—meat.

Black bears are omnivorous.

1

Black bears hibernate.

Glue bear's feet here.

Glue to the back of page one here.

Black bears sleep deeply in winter.

Black bears have five toes on each paw.

Black bears have toes!

2

Black bears can be brown, tan, a reddish color, or black.

Color.

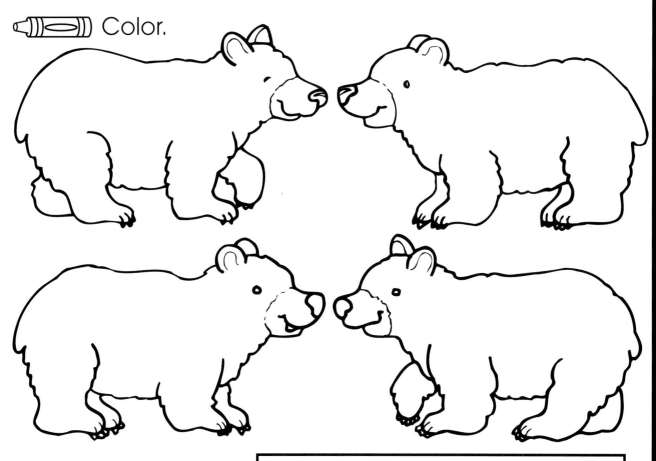

I know some words that tell about black bears.

Black bears are

3

Bear Bookmarks

Take this bookmark to the library to look for a bear book.

Bearman
Written by Laurence Pringle
Photographed by Lynn Rogers
Published by Charles Scribner's Sons

Good Morning, Granny Rose
Written & Illustrated by Warren Ludwig
Published by G. P. Putnam's Sons

How Do Bears Sleep?
Written & Illustrated by E. J. Bird
Published by Carolrhoda Books, Inc.

Eyewitness Juniors: Amazing Bears
Written by Theresa Greenaway
Photographed by Dave King
Published by Alfred A. Knopf, Inc.

Every Autumn Comes The Bear
Written & Illustrated by Jim Arnosky
Published by G. P. Putnam's Sons

Bears In The Forest
Written by Karen Wallace
Published by Candlewick Press

Alaska's Three Bears
Written by Shelly Gill
Illustrated by Shannon Cartwright
Published by Paws IV Publishing
  Company

This bookmark belongs to

Take this bookmark to the library to look for a bear book.

Bearman
Written by Laurence Pringle
Photographed by Lynn Rogers
Published by Charles Scribner's Sons

Good Morning, Granny Rose
Written & Illustrated by Warren Ludwig
Published by G. P. Putnam's Sons

How Do Bears Sleep?
Written & Illustrated by E. J. Bird
Published by Carolrhoda Books, Inc.

Eyewitness Juniors: Amazing Bears
Written by Theresa Greenaway
Photographed by Dave King
Published by Alfred A. Knopf, Inc.

Every Autumn Comes The Bear
Written & Illustrated by Jim Arnosky
Published by G. P. Putnam's Sons

Bears In The Forest
Written by Karen Wallace
Published by Candlewick Press

Alaska's Three Bears
Written by Shelly Gill
Illustrated by Shannon Cartwright
Published by Paws IV Publishing
  Company

This bookmark belongs to